Watching Cartoons Before Attending a Funeral

Watching Cartoons
Before Attending a Funeral

JOHN SUROWIECKI

WHITE PINE PRESS · BUFFALO, NEW YORK

WHITE PINE PRESS
P.O. Box 236, Buffalo, New York 14201
www.whitepine.org

ACKNOWLEDGMENTS: *Agnieszka's Dowry*: The Five Satins Play the Apocalypse. *Anthology*: Someone Who Looks Like Maurice Ravel. *Blue Mesa Review*: Summer in Nowhereville [Georgic No. 3]. *The Briar Cliff Review*: The Great Awakening in a Four-year-old Child. *Chiron Review*: Dinner with Villa-Lobos. *Columbia: A Journal of Literature and Art*: The Mermaid of Sag Harbor. *Common Ground Review*: Rumcake and Cookies at Mozzicato's. *Cream City Review*: My Life with the Virgin Mary. *Cumberland Poetry Review*: The Bookie's Wedding; Emptying A House; Loop for Attorney Szymanski. *Etcetera*: Two, Two, Two Infestations in One. *GSU Review*: Five-hundred Widowers in a Field of Chamomile. *Indiana Review*: Yale-New Haven, Mon Amour. *Kimera*: Someone from Spokane. *The Literary Review Web*: Proteus Poolside. *The MacGuffin*: Final Observations of the Incredible Shrinking Man. *The Mississippi Review*: Why Old Men Suddenly Break into Tears. *Nimrod International Journal*: Drought's End: Malambo. *North American Review*: Praying for Stalin's Death; On First Looking into a *Classics Illustrated* Homer. *Plainsongs*: Eaten Swans. *Poetry*: Our Cousin from Lublin. *Portland Pen*: The Mower at the VA Hospital. *Prairie Schooner*: Atomic Era Arias; JVVENAL; What It Means to Have X-ray Vision. *RHINO*: Watching Cartoons before Attending a Funeral. *Two Rivers Review*: Birds for My Mother. *2001: A Science Fiction Poetry Anthology*: Strange Nocturnal Transmissions from Planet X.

A number of the poems in this collection appeared in the chapbook, *Five-hundred Widowers in a Field of Chamomile*, published in 2002 by The Portlandia Group, Portland, Oregon.

I'd like to thank my son, John, and my daughter, Vanessa, for their unfailing love and support, and my dear friends, Barry and Mary Shapiro, for their encouragement. Also, I'd like to acknowledge the contribution made by the members of my softball team, The Fighting Plankton from Hell, who will be very surprised to learn that I write poetry.

Publication of this book was made possible, in part,
by public funds from the New York State Council on the Arts, a State Agency.

Printed and bound in the United States of America

First Edition

White Pine Press Poetry Prize, Number 8

Library of Congress Control Number: 2003100343

For Denise, with love.

CONTENTS

Watching Cartoons Before Attending a Funeral

Five-hundred Widowers in a Field of Chamomile

The yellow, the pollen, the millions of fallen petals
pull us down to sleep: all our dreams have gravity
like the one in which we are about to drift off
in our beds with the windows closed shut
and our wives reading in cones of yellow light,
their knees up like barricades, their eyes
smiling at a clever turn of phrase.

They sip their tea in unison and the tea starts
to smell like them, honey and wool, a musky odor
stolen from a gland like a tiny octagon of wax.
We sink deeper into our beds, into the earth:
the summer smells like sleep, is sleep,
its first instant, where everything is paired
and within reach and where it ought to be.

What It Means to Have X-ray Vision

This is the lovely world we seek out,
the steely seemingly moonlit world
where metal merits a black density
and flesh is a sitting pool of fog.

It only seems cold there, the blue
of icy lips, the icy ghosts of warm colors,
of matter and deception and levels
of fabrication. A swallow is beautiful,

as is a heartbeat and the glow of bone.
The sky is another kind of sky, another
kind of air, unbreathable, smothering,
rolled and scratched like a sheet of tin.

Sound is irrelevant, noise unheard of
and death well-marked: an inner fire
leaves a child marrowless, a hurricane's eye
touches down on an ocean of milk.

Dinner with Villa-Lobos

Cello-shaped Villa-Lobos arrives at seven-
thirty for pork and shrimp, ham and clams.
The French are the thieves of rhythm, having none
they can call their own. The violinophone is something
like a bowed zither; peripety is a feather in a gust of
wind. Uirapurú is love itself, an enchanted bird
impaled by the arrow of a beautiful woman.

The bird turns into a man who falls in love with
the aforementioned woman only to be killed by
mighty unromantic forces. He becomes the bird again,
only to die again at the woman's hand and so it
continues. Villa-Lobos is extravagant in his praise
of the flan and asks for the recipe which,
to his surprise, is not unlike any other.

Drive-by Elegy with Three Bullet Points

On the front page the candles appear larger
than life. The prose is knifelike: maybe it
can cut away the misery the light reveals.

·

Schoolgirls arrive at the EZ Mart to mourn,
to find his soul among the cliques of flies
that hover over loaves of whole-wheat bread,
to erect a monument of candles and cans.

·

The bullet was born in the last light of the first
steamy day, passed through his brain and came
to rest in a box of detergent, a slug in snow.

·

Later they are sorry to say they are most
sorry for candles melting and cans cashed in,
for people finding it difficult to remember him
or anyone's caring or a day too hot for May.

Summer in Nowhereville [Georgic No. 3]

There's nothing whatever to see
Except Polacks that pass in their motors
And play concertinas all night.
                    —Wallace Stevens

A rabbit hangs like Mussolini's mistress
under the skirt of its own skin.
They say its red blood makes blackberries.
They say blueberries turn your shit black.
Clouds harvest the breaths of babies
in whose cloudy eyes you can see the souls
of the recent dead. In gooseberries,
you can taste the sweet sweat of the insane.

Near pear-drunk bees we listen to European
orchestras and read about the underclass.
In their physics, an ordinary rain drowns
a sophisticated heart and summer seduces
with melon textures and jackets of minty air,
but they're silent on the subject of women
who crawl into bed on all fours, giddy
and wobbly and smelling of cherry brandy.

Watching Cartoons before Attending a Funeral

I
Astonished by blood's clownish color,
Bluto sits at the edge of the bed, his eyes
double-Xed and blue-and-gold like irises.

He eats his spinach, too, cans of the stuff,
but nothing ever happens. And this time
the world appears beyond rebuilding.

II
Olive's returned from a room with a view
of a suburban cul-de-sac. The maples
don't samba anymore and blue jays
don't hint at love's secrets. She asks
him to fasten her pearls,
to explain once again how death
is our taproot and our wings.

III

Finally he finds his only decent pair
of black shoes and explains how we flicker
and warp like a candle's shadow,
how we're ourselves and a map of ourselves,
how her half-swallowed yawns condemn

the babies she has glued together from bits
of magazines, how she's both bedroom
and bedroom light illuminating row after row
of wildflowers and cave swallows,
how the snapshot wedged into the edge

of her vanity mirror is a guard posted
between two worlds, how we're like music:
here, here in theory, here on paper,
here in a jukebox memory, here in the fire
that consumes a soul, but never here at all.

Loneliness Never Shuts Up

I sleep with him, an allegory, out of favor
for centuries. He blabs about everything:
my failings as a man, the carpenter ants' return,
the cheese gone bad. He talks through a concerto
as it scratches its way to our poor midnight
via a green-eyed radio; he even talks in my dreams
in which women glow like alarm-clock hands.

The word for today is *manumission*, as in:
I need to get my *m*. checked. As for spring,
as for crab trees in a red heat and pink phlox
spilling over lichened rocks, he could give a shit.
All he cares about are warm bodies:
he won't hear a word about the purity of Love
or the indispensability of Hope.

Why Old Men Suddenly Break into Tears

They think we have no hearts or have machines
for hearts: voltage regulators or hydraulic pumps.
They *become* hearts. They speak of sentiment as
a lapis egg, an unbreakable and pocketable jewel.

Anything starts them off: a tune, a gift, a TV show,
people who overcome adversity or demonstrate
our common humanity or some capacity for joy
or learn at long last the etiquette failure teaches.

Sometimes it's thinking how lucky they've been,
how they've done OK or done their part or how
the past is doomed to glimpses: an elm leafing,
an icehouse, a girl attempting a jackknife in July.

Atomic Era Arias

The Imperial Commissioner

After morning tea there are brief inquiries
masking fear and obligation and later on
there's the creak of a heron's wings
like an utterance of gratitude. A hole opens
in her chest and she looks like new butter
spilling off a plate.
                    She'd been the happiest
girl in Nagasaki. But because $\{\Lambda\}$ is a class
whose sole member is the empty class Λ
and nothing nothings, no time at all
had settled between a short nap and final rest.
She was eighteen. Agnus Dei: $\{\Lambda\}$ of God.

Suzuki

There was too much light at the threshold
of love, too much summer. Where her child
once played, monsters pick stars from the sky.
No one can bear the appearance of the place.
No one saw the ship arrive. Few were willing
to see it depart.
               Language is an ancient city,
a maze of streets and squares and houses;
the sciences are the suburbs of our language
and now there is nothing to say. We are all
lizards and locusts. *O ma un gel di morte vis ta.*
Her eyes glow like pearls in the moonlight.

Recluse at Nine O'clock

Most houses say something about someone;
his house asks only to be left alone.
It's a gray house, the color of shadow,
and so it seems big, the sum of the shadow
and it. If we're all houses, he is a house
within a house.

Mrs. Kogut is up and fetches the paper
in her curlers and Korean War kimono.
Through plaid scarves boys talk in excited
clouds about the triangle-stamp countries,
secretly watching for the sparkle of his eyes
in the glassblack.

Soon the cold arrives from colder towns
— Saskatoon, Slave Lake, Uranium City —
and the light falls in broad yellow sheets,
gilding the birdbones of his father's forsythias
and the side of his face he wouldn't mind
the world seeing.

Eaten Swans

Wonder what kind is swanmeat.
—Leopold Bloom

A circle of white ash remained and a tire iron,
which was the spit, and a mayonnaise jar
half-filled with meat cut into small pieces.
Factories were busy then, ball bearings,
cutlery, turbines, and people in town
were most thankful for what
they most despised.

Everyone knew what it was like to go hungry;
poetry had no power against desperation,
no urgency down to the dark red meat of the bone.
From each beak grew a tiny black rose of blood;
from each stomach spilled
the liquified remains
of everyone's bread.

Birds for My Mother

1

Their coos, caws and chick-a-dee-dee-dees
are all expressions of sympathy. She's their
gravity-bound, plumeless, tin-eared friend;
they take pity on her. A wren, for instance,
will carry her day on the fragile frame of its song,
a day of spaghetti in a can and ice cream in a cup.

2

I bring her coffee and lay out cupcakes in a ring.
I camp out under constellations of ceiling holes.
The world is a few rooms, a few crucifixes,
a few laminated articles on positive attitude.
She says a blue jay is nesting in her brain.
I hear a mourning dove.

3

The night buzzes on and off like a man with
throat cancer. Everything else is the quiet
an owl inspires. All night she hears leaves panic
and the air snap, filling vacuums. All night
she worries about her hummingbirds
and their last red drink before flying home.

Suicide at the Wheel

Prokofiev was on the radio when we raced
into the Haddam night; the highway lines
hit our brains like gunfire from a MiG-15.
Then it was lights off and utter blackness,
a fiction of stillness as we rushed headlong
into eternity. Images of dead shad came to mind,
of salt hay meadows and the apocalypse
of trees at Selden Creek, images of you
being pissed, you being pensive,

you sighing, you crying, you complaining,
you being dismissive, you wondering why you.
And when you turned on the headlights,
the roadside trees looked astonished;
a rabbit zigzagged in front of us, vanishing
into the cemetery you knew so well.
You were melancholy's favorite child:
one day you'd leave the world to darkness
and to me.

Poem about a Poem

Your poem is wrong in many ways.
My shoulders became a wall,
but only to block the morning light.

The moles on my back are not
a zodiac of dot-to-dot monsters,
all snoring, snorting and reptilian.

The light was golden, not dark gray.
The crows stayed for a minute or two
and weren't lined up like a panel of judges.

You didn't harvest bleeding hearts,
you didn't make me breakfast,
you don't own a cat

and the chickadee that crashed
into the window wasn't killed
and wasn't you.

Final Observations of the Incredible Shrinking Man

Our house is no larger than it ever was.
The stars aren't that much farther away,
just over six feet, practically nothing.

The hickory leaves are still peaked
like restaurant napkins; the church's spire
still points to the points of the moon.

Is it so different? Life shrinks, time shrinks,
death is the final sum: zero plus zero.
I see violets spit out their progeny,

I see that snails are their own spilled blood:
even the smallest mind imagines,
even the smallest heart yearns.

JVVENAL

Pasquinade for my brother.

Suddenly we are parentless
and to our surprise the world
embraces us, tips its gray fedora
and leaves unbroken our sad
string of cars. It has vodka

brought in and thirsty relatives
from Yonkers, fresh rye bread
and columns of ham tightly rolled.
It offers consolation and tears,
accompanying us to the library

for a J under the U-less names,
recalling how we used to look up
ancient poets and girls' dresses
and fuse the great mysteries
with our spit. It will throw up

on its wingtips and pass out
in the pool room, coming to when
kind words lose their authority
and affection turns fraudulent
and we are two pillars of stone.

Her Cough Sounds Like a Dog's Bark

I can see her lungs as she smokes an L&M
under a faded Cinzano umbrella: they look
like black oven mitts. Cottonball clouds
make it look like Maine in September, but it's
the middle of nowhere in the middle of
                              March

and her life is a debt no one will assume,
a consuming smokiness. I see her heart
spasm and flip-flop like a bass on a dock.
I see the cancer in her throat and she is
so deathly afraid of it she refuses to say its
                              name.

Her coughing makes the lunchtime crowd
look for a barking dog beyond her umbrella,
the same dog that keeps them awake and makes
them realize how little they have to do with
anyone's pity or concern. When windows (triple-
ply

glass) and walls of arborvitae don't muffle
the barking, they become grateful for
the first smudge of dog-tongue-pink light,
as grateful as they are now that they had
never been and could never be anyone like
                              her.

The Great Awakening in a Four-year-old Child

At length, she suddenly ceased crying,
and began to smile and presently said...
Mother, the kingdom of heaven is come to me.
                                        —Jonathan Edwards

In hell, she saw a lagoon filled with the tears
she'd shed at night and larders filled with fat
blue plums no one ate because they'd been stolen.
And since every family was poor, no one,
by definition, could be charitable or of help.

Heaven had something to do with largeness,
eye-level daffodils and corn, outsized moths
with mother-of-pearl wings sleeping in her shoes,
snoring, she said; also, with largess.
Presents were everywhere, behemoth dolls

spilling over chairs, spaniels in crawl spaces,
spotted ponies trotting in circles. Heaven
was the snow-crushed world springing back,
a forest of oaks on the verge of leafing,
thick with animals on the verge of song.

The Five Satins Play the Apocalypse

> Still was the night, serene and bright,
> when all men sleeping lay.
> —Michael Wigglesworth,
> The Day of Doom [1662]

We're bedazzled and UV-purple in a gym
the size of the world when suddenly they
appear in sequined black and spit-
polished shoes of Army issue: four angels
and a pickup sax announcing the end of history
and the beginning of remembering.

My rented tuxedo and I subdue
an erection in the final slow dance of time,
an inching of soles across center court,
the enormous river of us all: all elected,
all spaced-out and spacebound, all grooving
to the still center of the B-side night.

The Mermaid of Sag Harbor

She unmendeleevs you. In her room
she keeps vials, flasks, inks, potions,
something like a centrifuge holding rollers.
Her bed is an eddy of sheets, hissing from salt.
The blue of sea kings shines through her skin.
She's the adventuress in a sinking house,
entertained by jewelry and lines of coke.

She asks for warmth against warmth
generating new warmth and has nothing
more to say except how warm the warmth is
or how quiet the quiet is or how mighty
the night winds are that shred the cafe flags.
Sea urchins are the coins of her mistrust;
gulls chart for her a geography of exits.

Variation on a Tree by V. Nabokov

How accessible ether! How easy flight!

When she climbed her backyard tree
it had limbs like an Octopus ride and its
France-shaped leaves were half-eaten
by bugs. When it became clear to us
she'd never return, we met for drinks
and with the sun in our eyes recalled

how the night was a lens over her house,
shifting powers; how voices, familiar
and then not, spilled from the lacy
beckoning of her kitchen windows;
how she thought of herself as a sample

of earth, a cylinder of earthworms;
how she vanished, bequeathing us
clouds that looked like her or her girls
or her ex or a heartsick country with
its coast reforming and its estuary
a wound suddenly healing.

Exodus of the Heroin Addicts

They are a river exiting, headed for the suburbs.
Our irises are lovely purple ladies to them.
Our daylilies are undersized and pale,
but they don't seem to mind. They lean
on their rakes and talk about warming trends.
The terrible years are behind them. They see
the journey as necessary and inevitable:
all along they wanted to live here, to be like us,

to be compassionate and generous and fair.
They see junkies as leaves trapped in privets,
unable to rise above the lowest rungs of air.
They see the afternoon sun as a talisman,
the moon as a novella about first loves
and the harmless indiscretions of the heart.
They give generously to cancer research.
Their daughters are bound for college.

Loop for Attorney Szymanski

Young men touch his yellow convertible
thinking in all fairness it should be theirs.
He drives it to the track, Yonkers mostly,
or to the beach where he inspects men's catches
and asks about their wives.

He finds a spot among the dunes,
a spiraling of self upon self upon self,
and listens to screams from the roller coaster.
He orders fried clams and stabs at their bellies
with a wooden prong, watching water bead

on a young girl's legs. His teeth are gray
from eating licorice and lean this way and that
like slabs in a Puritan cemetery. When he's not
eating licorice, his teeth are yellow,
but not the yellow of his car.

The Mower at the VA Hospital

I

Our mower is young and broad-shouldered:
so were we. Love confuses him as it once did us;
the pain he feels he believes to be genuine.
He even believes it to be pain.
The tiny pink man from Verdun has shit his bed,
the handless man scratches his face like a housecat,
the mower mows and our grief is where it was.

II

We remember some things, but nothing
so exact as form or color or disposition.
All day the wards are dark, while night wears
paper shoes and speaks in insect languages.
Its milky light is sticky and inescapable;
it seals us up. Death is also a mower,
but our mower doesn't know a thing about death.

III

Our corpses are the color of plain black shoes
or white cotton socks: now you know what
never did become of us after all these years.
The lawns are littered with debris from
a summery war of winds; our mower will grind it
into dust. Before him: a meadow, a stream, a city,
all sliced into colors like a snake.

IV

Tonight, stung by love, our mower will repeat
his curves and rows, his stars and spine aligned.
For us: zitis and marinara begotten by despair
upon impossibility. In the lobby, the news
goes unwatched; a last wave agitates the air.
In the B canteen, a small profit is made
in Camels and Juicy Fruit gum.

Our Cousin from Lublin

For Dennis and Gloria.

After finishing off the bottle of vodka he says
life is everything children are ignorant of,
including us, their heroes, who become small
and replaceable. And while remorse
pricks us like holly leaves, history does not.
A map of his country

looks like a human face, a round
and ordinary face, tear-carved
and marked by the dead with their graffiti
of scratched initials and pleas for air.
The map is also the memory of an empire:
as if the face were overwhelmed by a large hat.

He remembers the mural of a saint and how
the landscape looked suspiciously like Italy:
olive trees, fig trees, a basilica. The saint's beard
resembled a caterpillar nest and crowded under
his cloak were the children of the saved, painted
to lock eyes with the children of the poor.

He says vodka is a river and maybe the sea
and they swim in it like children with blue lips
and the shakes, waiting for life to overwhelm
its metaphors. People in Kiev are paid in vodka
and more vodka and assurances that wealth
has nothing to do with money.

The Bookie's Wedding

He's chosen sweetness over risk,
a quiet girl who plays the piano quietly.
We no longer notice the artful passes
that kept a mole and then its scar
in the shadow of her hand.

Her mother is a garden in autumn,
a reddish sinking in the ground.
She wears her hard life as rouge.
Extending her cold hand coldly,
she won't serve the good wine at all.

Rung glasses don't summon kisses.
The flowers are already on their weary
airborne way to spring. The aunts
dance in circles circumspectly;
the uncles remain close to death.

The groom leans against the wall
like a poolstick. There are no sums,
no remainders, only means endlessly.
The Knicks are laid waste:
who will bemoan them?

My Life with the Virgin Mary

1

Always the blue veil, the blue sky,
the blue countenance, the black serpent
between her ivory toes pleading for
a gloss on the power that keeps it there.
Her panties: also blue.

2

Never have I seen the white of her teeth.
I tumble stillborn out of the confessional,
the curtain groping at my ankles,
and all I see is a thin unsmiling
black line between her lips.

3

I have sinned, I have sinned:
I have drawn chalk pricks on red bricks
for all the nuns to see. I must be less filthy,
more obedient, better: her ocean, out of pity,
can interpose with doom.

4

She's happy to destroy my enemies,
a breath to her, a hurricane to them.
Only I taste her garlicky descent,
the salt of her helplessness,
the living yeast of her love.

5

In my bed, I find crumbs of talcum paste
among the coffee-colored spots above
her roseolar breasts. She points out
midnight at noon: the sleeping moth
like a seashell glued to a tree.

6

She races through winters, light-devouring,
blue-lipped, coughing up yellow pellets.
In the summer, light must find her
through walls of ice, blue as
forget-me-nots and trembling.

Praying for Stalin's Death

We were asked to pray for Stalin's death
and then one day he died. Only the nuns
were jubilant, swatches of void and white
under a Roman-numeral clock. We were
their metastasizing agents, transmitters
of harmless-at-first discolorations and bumps.

Then his lungs collapsed; his blood flowed
like minestrone. Apparently, we were
the conspirators he'd been so afraid of;
we penetrated his dreams waving red hands
from inside a hole in the ground. Not much later
sleep with quiet malice would stop his heart.

Three Things Sophie Likes

She likes saying she's gone soft-headed,
spongy as an eggplant, weeping beads
that stain her pillow and give it a buttery smell.
When she wakes up her head feels like it's
been kneaded and hammered until it
looks like a baked scallop or the Guggenheim.

She likes visitors and she'll look at your chest
hoping to find a name. Then she'll show off
her sunny yellow room with photos
tucked in frames like boats in dry dock
and doilies and lampshades frilled
like oystermeat. She likes talking about

the horseshoes at St. Mary's Beach, her hubcap
armada with plates gull-jimmied and dagger-
tails undone. She says they're not really crabs,
you know, but a species of sea spider.
And they're hard, very hard, and torpedo-
headed as time seems to be or inevitability.

On *First Looking into a* Classics Illustrated *Homer*

Zeus and I loved her: Athene: gorgeous,
brainy, statuesque, forehead-born.
Full-fleshed in a paradise of olive groves
and caper bushes and bank colonnades,

she was by the Kong-high gates of Troy
a dotted-line invisibility in Empire décolletage.
She was a true comix queen: placative
and privy to thunderbolts and ideas.

Achilles deferred to her, Diomedes struck
a god under her aegis. I would have been
her slave, given her the golden apple
and ended the war before it began.

Proteus Poolside

He can be himself, a short, impatient man
with nothing to do on a Saturday afternoon,
or he can be an impermanent stillness,
a breeze carrying the shouts of children
and a hint of cooking. He can be a tirade
in the cause of privacy, a plea for compassion,
a patch of Indian mustard drawing poisons
from common dirt.

              He can be a chrysalis
or a fresh cutting in a bed-smelling room.
He can be the sea, a seal in the sea, the pool
or the girl coming out of the pool pulling at
her crack and pounding water out of her ear.
He can be the woman she becomes, the young
mother he finds so appealing or the young man
who so appeals to her.

              He can be a fly, a public
official, a gutter chicory, an old friend in
the restaurant business, a solitary crow
or the sparrow chasing it, a blue cabbage,
a blue, a cabbage moth, a pie baked by a
librarian, a whiff of chlorine, a drop of iodine,
a sky-mirroring morning glory, the sky,
a season.

Poseidon Turns Up in Point Judith, R.I.

He's up at last, half-blind in the sunroom,
still mooning over Medusa and wondering
if the clams are OK. The sea is an ungodly
shade of brown: oil-slick rainbows ride it
and a sickly blue smoke clings to it.

It all went bad when snakes began popping out
of her head. That was when he turned to stone,
turned against what he was, his medium,
his blood, spilling into a world where
beauty can become vile and hideous.

He watches the ferry depart, recalling monsters
dragged ashore for children to marvel at
and women to gut. He waves at the weekend
birders as they test the brief cages of their
Swiss lenses, then at the lovers holding hands.

Eclogue for a Taxidermist

When Walt's calf was barbecue black,
the barn owl unfolded above the sofa-
bed turned pulpy and the back-glancing fox
just stared at the wall and when he died

the whole house became gangrenous:
the raven collapsed into soot, the brookie,
twisting, twisting, pulled free of its board
and like Walt's soul jumped out the window.

Strange Nocturnal Transmissions from Planet X

A rain of rays pricks the night like firefly amours.
Peonies unravel, drugstore chocolates overflow
their pleated paper cups. I hear the rustle of pages
and the deep sighs that conclude both work and sex.
And I hear you

telling me that the lonely heart is a knot or fist
or stone or lump of coal with built-in heat and hope
of someone descending, that a lonely day is filled
with retreats and reappraisals of pain's inarguable face,
that the end of love

is the end of the world and that the world is you,
beyond the hickories, lovely and civilizing. Lumps
of infinity form in my throat. If I sleep, if I sleep
with you, I'm a goner, and a whole new me
will form in your bed.

Nothingness Becomes Her

She's something all right, cold as the sea,
a ship's figurehead cutting through the night,
breasts and chin jutted out. Naked, she walks
on tiptoe; fully clothed, she walks like a sailor,
afraid of nothing, unafraid of nothingness.
Every step she takes is a tile in a mosaic
that, for us, will have to pass for earth.

Love isn't for her: the heart is the fat-fringed
organ cooks use for gravy. She says joy
is the idea of joy, all we have of joy,
joy enough since joy exempts.
She has no talent for sympathy
and no capacity for sorrow:
if she did it would all fall apart.

Someone Who Looks Like Maurice Ravel

Into the left hand of a radio sonata slips
the in-key hum of an old prop plane;
he likes the fit of it, not the serendipity,
never that: but it's February and there isn't

much to do. Shirt pressed, tie Orphistic,
a silken shingling of circles, he looks like
a waiter, as did the maestro, snow-haired
and tuxedoed, in the Pathé News,

a prisoner, he says, of his own refinement,
"artificial by nature," a humble architect
of games and diversions, good with kids,
but not a whore to their delight. Sunlight

lingers in the hothouse of his kitchen,
urging plants, African and elephant-
eared, to wildness, which he, cutting back
and reshaping, won't allow. The teakettle

sounds like a train whistle as waxwings,
having come and gone that morning
before he could find his binoculars,
find him unprepared again.

Someone from Spokane

The world introduces its emissaries:
Queensland ginger, Zante currants.
Clam-colored light stops at her sink,
content to eavesdrop. Alder rubs
at her bay windows, the ice-cube maker
thumps and she sings her few lovely notes.
She bakes a pie and cuts it into
as many slices as she has people over.

Her husband liked her pies. His hair
was like the strips of paper fluttering
in front of the new air conditioners at Sears.
Back east, a mockingbird once repeated
the whistle she used to call in the cat.
He liked it that the cat obeyed like a dog.
This was at a time when she
didn't need any friends.

She knew he'd been the mockingbird.
He'd been the Atlantic as well, his fists
uncurling, another pair of obedient
hands to support the jittery voyages
beyond the strung lights and shore cafes.
He'd carried himself to his own end
and the world became a circle of friends:
an unfathomable blue pie.

Drought's End: Malambo

The heat has soured her stomach
and yellowed the sweetpea's heart.
It has made the cat sing in its sleep,
dreaming of anything but the dust
that hides inside every breath.

The heat has made her a little nuts.
Dirt finds the creases of her wrists,
throat, the fulcrums of her elbows.
She won't be touched or spoken to.
And then there are her migraines.

Suddenly, salvation rains down
on our cukes and zukes, anthills
return to loam and inside our bodies
our hearts wiggle like JELL-O
reconstituted from a brick-red dust.

Yale-New Haven, Mon Amour

Diane: In memoriam.

1

It has two forms: as tumor
and interstitially throughout.
It is: the size of a human eye
and it looks milky like an eye.
It is: a field of snow a brief
forgotten wind has marked.

It is: not a rust, not an eroder,
but a lungfire burning. It is:
solid in tissue, liquid in pleura,
vaporous in breath. It belittles:
each common breath is a stage
aside ridiculing her. It grows.

It advances. The seasons turn,
days shorten and light thins.

2

Because her gums often bleed
she brushes with bicarbonate,
gently, gently, releasing a drop

of opal and ruby into a kidney-
shaped cup, tilting her head,
a woman in a Degas with

bathroom light flying at her in gobs,
a beautiful towel-turbaned woman
at her toilette, preparing for love

or an afternoon in the country
where the light is so brilliant
and salutary, it has a life of its own.

3

When I say I think of her I mean
to say I see her raking leaves
on a cold October day. Where
there is blue, van Gogh noted,
there is yellow, or ought to be,
and so there was on that particular day
with that particularly blue sky
and those remaining yellow leaves
which she wished had fallen
with the neatly raked others:
the shimmer of opposites, of life.

4

In her cancer books, all things
are perfectible and all perfections
are beyond debate. October clouds
form a calendar with numbers
in the corners and jotted notes
explaining what has to be done.
The nurses laugh, as they must,
but it's still painful to hear.

Enter: by a triangular room,
as if hope so dim didn't warrant
a completing wall, continue to
hemodialysis and the hallway
of bad art and pass the solarium
where the day before she strained
for breath and finally did not
she last touched sunlight.

Emptying a House

The day I put aside the black searches
for a vein and the nightly encounters
with her perfume, a book spills out
a note requesting books in a scrawl
that's still impatient. The walls are

indifferent tissue, the hardwood floors
hold a tiny smudge of light and a last fork
finds its fork-shaped slot. Square glasses
will no longer surprise those children
who don't think to use the corners.

There are racks of clothes to give away,
jewels to silence in a black velvet bag.
Documents are wrapped in red ribbon.
In the fridge, there's a carton of juice;
in the crisper, a failed pharmacy.

Two Chemists

Aleksandr Borodin

An amateur cares about loveliness;
everything else is ordinary life.
Organic chemistry is like music:
from a finite scale, infinite variations,
although always in the key of C.
When music is played, everything
reconnects and reconfigures.
You hear the melody of atoms;
a birch has its song, so has a moth
and a cloud passing overhead
and a cat napping in a chair.

Primo Levi

An amateur needs to write it all
down before it all falls apart
— the story of bonds cracking
and valences shifting, of metals
turning ignoble and the ocean
turning into hydrogen peroxide:
sputtering, hissing, working up
an appetite for blood. Survival
is an abstract, a preface, a few
anecdotes about the elements,
a parable about the dark.

Two, Two, Two Infestations in One

Ladybugs

They say: Fly in a series of cursive e's,
settle in unsettled colonies and be good,
be kind, be generous and be small
and insignificant as you sit at your
kitchen table close to the stove with its low

blue flame spread out like a dandelion
and recall putting on a hat in Hartford
or getting into a car with someone you loved
at a time when you glowed with promise
and she was indifferent to success.

Flies

They say: Cover things like a black mitten,
a panhandle, for instance, or a salt shaker
or form a helixing black molecule along
a kitchen light string.

          Then rub vitamin E
on your skin for a lifelike luster and don't
worry about lumps or fits of coughing.

          You
have l-o-v-e to offer strength and protection,
to drip, drip, drip away the pain of life. You
have l-o-v-e to inspire bold deeds, l-o-v-e
to remember when you don't remember h-e-r.

The Decline of the Silverware Industry in Connecticut

Behind the vitriol-blue windows,
fork embryos emerge from their baths
and evaporated sweat forms clouds
in the rafters, soon to rain down on us,
a rain that smells like us and is as hot
as we are. We line up for salt pills to kill
a quarter of an hour. We ask questions
because it takes time to ask questions.

In the open stalls we dream of their blossom-
scented wives, their lives in ruin, their houses
in collapse, with bathtubs howling and wallpaper
fluttering like the flags of a humbled army.
And every day women clock out with silver
in their vaginas, a full set by Christmas,
dipped and polished and then put away
in a satin bed for a marriage's first meal.

Rumcake and Cookies at Mozzicato's

For Denise.

Love is a hunger and a dessert, a golden cake
wet with rum or madeleines reserved for
the unrelenting showers of unrelenting afternoons.
Our oaths, made in winter, parade two by two
across the marbletop counter. The waiter nods.

Love is caramelization and saturation: changes
in the weather, in the chemistry of things.
Soon spring will seem ordinary and we'll be tired of
losing sleep. Then a quiet enthusiasm goes into effect
which, the waiter says, is another season.

The White Pine Press Poetry Prize

Vol. 8   *Watching Cartoons Before Attending a Funeral* by John Surowiecki
Selected by C.D. Wright

Vol. 7.   *My Father Sings, to My Embarrassment* by Sandra Castillo
Selected by Cornelius Eady

Vol. 6   *If Not for These Wrinkles of Darkness* by Stephen Frech
Selected by Pattiann Rogers

Vol. 5   *Trouble in History* by David Keller
Selected by Pablo Medina

Vol. 4   *Winged Insects* by Joel Long
Selected by Jane Hirshfield

Vol. 3   *A Gathering of Mother Tongues* by Jacqueline Joan Johnson
Selected by Maurice Kenny

Vol. 2   *Bodily Course* by Deborah Gorlin
Selected by Mekeel McBride

Vol. 1   *Zoo & Cathedral* by Nancy Johnson
Selected by David St. John